# THE JESUS LIFESTYLE

## SERIES TWO

## NICKY GUMBEL

Published by Alpha International

Holy Trinity Brompton, Brompton Road, London SW7 1JA

publications@alpha.org

# CONTENTS

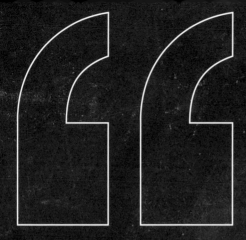

*Again, you have heard that it was said to the people long ago, 'Do not break your oath, but keep the oaths you have made to the Lord.'*

*But I tell you, do not swear at all: either by heaven, for it is God's throne; or by the earth, for it is his footstool; or by Jerusalem, for it is the city of the Great King. And do not swear by your head, for you cannot make even one hair white or black.*

*Simply let your 'Yes' be 'Yes', and your 'No', 'No'; anything beyond this comes from the evil one.*

MATTHEW
5:33-37

# how to **live** and **act** with **integrity**

## INTRODUCTION

Many people struggle with integrity. Lying is considered acceptable, resulting in a breakdown of trust in society.

Why is integrity so important?

Integrity is the key to:

- Strong **personal relationships** (Exodus 18:16-18, *The Message*)

- Long-term **success** (Proverbs 11:3)

- Good **leadership** (Proverbs 20:28, *The Message*)

- **Pleasing God** (1 Chronicles 29:17)

# 1

## LIVE A CONSISTENT LIFE
## WITHOUT COMPARTMENTS
## – INTEGRITY OF LIFE

> **Again, you have heard that it was said to the people long ago, 'Do not break your oath, but keep the oaths you have made to the Lord.'**

**MATTHEW 5:33**

> **But I tell you, do not swear at all: either by heaven, for it is God's throne; or by the earth, for it is his footstool; or by Jerusalem, for it is the city of the Great King. And do not swear by your head, for you cannot make even one hair white or black.**

**MATTHEW 5:34-36**

Jesus confronts the corrupt system of oath-taking and reminds us that God sees the whole of our lives.

- Avoid the 'titanic' mistake

  - God should be at the centre of our lives

  - every aspect of our lives – work, home, church, and social life – should be integrated with our faith in God

- Apply the 'front page' test

  - success begins with personal integrity

  - the truth will always be disclosed

**LUKE 8:17**

# 2

## SPEAK THE TRUTH WITHOUT DECEPTION – INTEGRITY OF WORDS

**“** Simply let your 'Yes' be 'Yes', and your 'No', 'No'; anything beyond this comes from the evil one. **”**

**MATTHEW 5:37**

**“** If you always tell the truth, you don't have to remember what you said. **”**

*Mark Twain*

Jesus said **“** I am ... the truth. **”**

**JOHN 14:6**

- Speak the truth in love

**EPHESIANS 4:15**

  - we should not be rude; always gracious

  - sometimes we do have to confront, but only in love

NOTES

# 3

## CULTIVATE A PURE HEART WITHOUT FAKING IT – INTEGRITY OF HEART

**❝** 'Teacher', [the Pharisees] said, 'we know you are a man of integrity and that you teach the way of God in accordance with the truth. You aren't swayed by men, because you pay no attention to who they are.' **❞**

**MATTHEW 22:16**

Treat everyone the same regardless of who they are.

**❝** David shepherded them with integrity of heart. **❞**

**PSALM 78:72**

True integrity is when our lives, our words and our hearts are all in alignment.

Integrity is doing the right thing even when no one is watching.

Be **REAL** by:

- Repenting
  - keep short accounts with God
- Enjoying God's favour
  - God offers forgiveness, no matter what we have done
- Aiming high
  - aim to live life with integrity at all times, always striving for the best
- Living by the Spirit
  - we need the help of the Spirit; we need new hearts

# ONCLUSION

The challenge is to live with our whole lives surrendered to the lordship of Christ.

❝ When Jesus is Lord of our beliefs, opinions, ambitions, standards, values and lifestyle, then we are integrated Christians. Then integrity marks our life. Only when he is Lord do we become whole. ❞
*John Stott*

NOTES

# DISCUSSION QUESTIONS

**1.** Have you had any recent experience of dishonesty in others? How did it make you feel?

**2.** What opportunities have you had recently to show integrity?

**3.** Jesus said, 'Simply let your "Yes" be "Yes", and your "No", "No"' (Matthew 5:37). If you were to follow this teaching, what difference would it make in your everyday life?

**4.** What are some of the challenges to integrity faced by Christians in our society today? How could these obstacles be overcome?

**5.** Jesus sets the bar very high in this area. He is 'a man of integrity and ... teach[es] the way of God in accordance with the truth'. Jesus isn't 'swayed by men' (Matthew 22:16). Why do you think this is? How can we try to achieve a level of integrity that is closer to Jesus'?

**6.** In our Christian communities, how can we help each other to live with integrity and be role models for others?

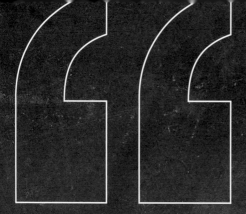

You have heard that it was said, 'Eye for eye, and tooth for tooth.' But I tell you, do not resist an evil person.

If someone strikes you on the right cheek, turn to him the other also.

And if someone wants to sue you and take your tunic, let him have your cloak as well.

If someone forces you to go one mile, go with him two miles.

Give to the one who asks you, and do not turn away from the one who wants to borrow from you.

MATTHEW
5:38-42

# how to **respond** to **difficult** people

## INTRODUCTION

How should we respond when we are **wronged?**

What did Jesus mean when he said, **❝ do not resist an evil person ❞** ?
**MATTHEW 5:39**

We should avoid the interpretations which lead to:

- **Literalism** (Leo Tolstoy)

- **Rejection** (Friedrich Nietzsche)

So what is Jesus saying?

# 1

## EXPECT TO ENCOUNTER DIFFICULT PEOPLE

- Those who are rude, insulting and abusive

  - loss of pride

    **❝ If someone strikes you on the right cheek, turn to him the other... ❞**
    **MATTHEW 5:39**

- Those who persecute or even prosecute

  - loss of possessions

    **❝ If someone wants to sue you and take your tunic, let him have your cloak as well ... ❞**
    **MATTHEW 5:40**

- Those who waste your time

  - loss of time

    **❝ If someone forces you to go one mile, go with him two miles. ❞**
    **MATTHEW 5:41**

- Those who are takers

  - loss of money

    **❝ ... do not turn away from the one who wants to borrow from you. ❞**
    **MATTHEW 5:42**

So how do we respond to these kind of people?

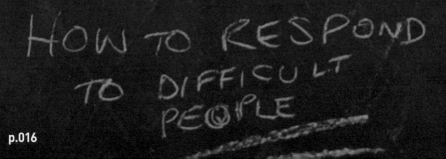

HOW TO RESPOND TO DIFFICULT PEOPLE

NOTES

# 2 RISE ABOVE TAKING REVENGE

> **"** You have heard that it was said 'Eye for eye, and tooth for tooth.' **"**
> **MATTHEW 5:38**

Jesus does not contradict the teaching in the Old Testament; rather, he speaks against its misinterpretation and misapplication.

## Four qualifications:

- Restrictive rather than permissive
  - punishment should fit the crime

- For judges, not private individuals
  - guide for judges in sentencing

- Rarely taken literally
  - except in the case of capital offences (similar to our legal system)

- Not the whole picture
  - even as far as the Old Testament is concerned

**PROVERBS 24**

Jesus forbids revenge, but there is nothing passive about his examples of non-retaliation:

- **"** ... turn the other cheek ... **"**
  **MATTHEW 5:39**
  - actively engage to overcome evil with good

- **"** Hand over your cloak as well ... **"**
  **MATTHEW 5:40**
  - take initiative

- **"** ... go two miles ... **"**
  **MATTHEW 5:41**
  - turn the tables

- **"** Give to the one who asks you, and do not turn away ... **"**
  **MATTHEW 5:42**
  - change the dynamics

HOW TO RESPON TO DIFFICULT PEOPLE

# 3 ACT WITH AN ATTITUDE OF RADICAL LOVE

We have to interpret Jesus' teaching in the context of everything else he did and said, and in light of the rest of the New Testament.

### Jesus:

- Drove out the money changers
  **JOHN 2:13-16**

- Verbally attacked scribes and Pharisees **MATTHEW 23**

- Demanded an explanation of physical abuse **JOHN 18:23**

### Paul:

- Refused to allow the authorities to act illegally **ACTS 16:37**

- Enforced his rights
  **ACTS 22:25; ACTS 25:8-12**

- Taught distinction between dealings of state and personal morality
  **ROMANS 13:1-4**

The state, as well as ourselves as Christian citizens, may need to use force to restrain evil and protect others. But as individuals, we must always act in love and rise above revenge. Both of these are principles of love.

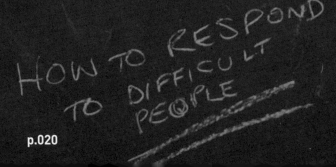

HOW TO RESPOND TO DIFFICULT PEOPLE

# ONCLUSION

Jesus calls us to disregard our own rights, but be passionate about the rights of others.

**❝ IT LOOKED AS THOUGH EVIL HAD TRIUMPHED ON THE CROSS, BUT THE REAL VICTORY BELONGED TO JESUS. THE CROSS IS THE ONLY POWER IN THE WORLD WHICH PROVES THAT SUFFERING LOVE CAN AVENGE AND VANQUISH EVIL. ❞**

*Dietrich Bonhoeffer*

NOTES

# DISCUSSION QUESTIONS

**1.** What kind of people do you find most difficult to deal with? When you encounter them, how do you usually respond? How would you like to respond?

**2.** What does Jesus mean when he says 'do not resist an evil person' (Matthew 5:39)? Why is this important?

**3.** In everyday life, what does it mean to 'turn the other cheek' (Matthew 5:39)?

**4.** Jesus gives four situations in which his followers are not to seek revenge. Can you think of modern equivalents for these?

**5.** How can we start to act with an attitude of radical love? How would this affect those who are rude to us, and in turn, society in general?

**6.** What can we do to avoid being a 'difficult person'? Have there ever been times when you were the one in the wrong? How did others react to you then? How did you rectify the situation?

*You have heard that it was said, 'Love your neighbour and hate your enemy.' But I tell you: love your enemies and pray for those who persecute you, that you may be sons of your Father in heaven. He causes his sun to rise on the evil and the good, and sends rain on the righteous and the unrighteous.*

*If you love those who love you, what reward will you get? Are not even the tax collectors doing that? And if you greet only your own people, what are you doing more than others? Do not even pagans do that? Be perfect, therefore, as your heavenly Father is perfect.*

MATTHEW
5:43-48

# how to **handle** **conflict**

# INTRODUCTION

We live in a **divided world**.

> **❝** The Bible tells us to love our neighbours but also to love our enemies, probably because they're generally the same people. **❞**
>
> *G.K. Chesterton*

God created us to have a loving relationship with him and with other people. This is not always easy; relationships can be difficult. If we want to achieve anything for God, we are likely to arouse enmity.

> **❝** You have heard that it was said, 'Love your neighbour and hate your enemy.' But I tell you: love your enemies ... **❞**
>
> **MATTHEW 5:43-44A**

Loving our enemies takes **initiative, strength and courage**.

# 1 SPEAK GRACIOUSLY

# 2 RESPOND KINDLY

**❝ Bless those who curse you … ❞**
**MATTHEW 5:44 – A LATER MANUSCRIPT,**
**SEE NIV FOOTNOTE AND LUKE 6:28**

*Eulogo* (Greek) – to bless, speak well of, praise or extol.

**❝ Bless those who persecute you; bless and do not curse. ❞**
**ROMANS 12:14**

We always need to speak well of our enemies, not only to their faces, but also behind their backs.

Jesus is the supreme example of someone who spoke graciously.

**❝ … do good to those who hate you. ❞**
**MATTHEW 5:44 – A LATER MANUSCRIPT,**
**SEE NIV FOOTNOTE AND LUKE 6:27**

*Kalos* (Greek) – to act beautifully.

This is the opposite of revenge and retaliation, which multiply hate and destroy us.

Non-retaliation transforms relationships.

**❝ Do not repay anyone evil for evil. Be careful to do what is right in the eyes of everybody. If it is possible, as far as it depends on you, live at peace with everyone. ❞**
**ROMANS 12:17-18**

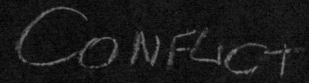

NOTES

# 3 PRAY POSITIVELY

# 4 ACT DIVINELY

**❝ ... and pray for those who persecute you ... ❞**

**MATTHEW 5:44**

Jesus encourages us to intercede for our enemies.

Jesus himself prayed for those who tortured him:

**❝ Father, forgive them, for they do not know what they are doing. ❞**

**LUKE 23:34**

**❝ To return hate for love is demonic, to return love for love, that is human. To return love for hate, that's divine. ❞**

God's love extends to those who are hostile towards him.

**❝ ... that you may be children of your Father in heaven. He causes his sun to rise on the evil and the good, and sends rain on the righteous and the unrighteous. ❞**

**MATTHEW 5:45**

God's blessings are indiscriminate and his grace is available to everyone.

Jesus asks us to look at people as God does.

CONFLICT

NOTES

# 5 LIVE DIFFERENTLY

**❝** If you love those who love you, what reward will you get? Are not even the tax collectors doing that? And if you greet only your own people, what are you doing more than others? Do not even pagans do that? **❞**

**MATTHEW 5:46-47**

As Christians, we have to be different. We have to do 'more than' others.

Why? Because we believe that there is a God who will judge.

**❝** Do not take revenge, my friends, but leave room for God's wrath, for it is written: 'It is mine to avenge; I will repay,' says the Lord. On the contrary: 'If your enemies are hungry, feed them; if they are thirsty, give them something to drink. In doing this, you will heap burning coals on their heads.' Do not be overcome by evil, but overcome evil with good. **❞**

**ROMANS 12:19-21**

We see this:

- In the life of Jesus, who trusted in God to deliver him on the cross

- Foreshadowed in the Old Testament in the life of Joseph

**❝** Do you yearn for the moment of vengeance, for the moment when everyone will see the truth? Of course you do ... the wisest thing one can ever do when mistreated is to be quiet about it. Joseph kept quiet. God wanted him to lose the battle so he might win the war ... there are unseen reasons for continued suffering. Who knows what God will do with your life if you take your mistreatment with dignity? **❞**

*R.T. Kendall*

# CONCLUSION

> ❝ Be perfect, therefore, as your heavenly Father is perfect. ❞
>
> **MATTHEW 5:48**

The challenge is to strive to be perfect in relationships; in love for our friends and our enemies.

How is this possible?

### 1. Easter

Through the cross; because we know we have been forgiven. When we know how much we have been forgiven, we know that we cannot hold anything against anyone else.

### 2. Pentecost

The love of God is poured into our hearts by the Holy Spirit.

NOTES

# DISCUSSION QUESTIONS

**1.** How do you usually deal with conflict?

**2.** Which of the five practical ways to love your enemies do you identify with (or feel represents your reaction to conflict) most closely? How often do you naturally employ these techniques? Can you think of an example?

**3.** Do you have an enemy who needs your prayers? What would it be like praying for them?

**4.** We read in the Bible that we should '... overcome evil with good' (Romans 12:21). In today's violent world, how might that lead Christians to live differently to others?

**5.** How could you start to employ the five practical ways to love your enemies? What steps could you take to ensure these 'positive' ways become your default reactions?

**6.** Think of a recent incident when you didn't handle conflict well. Keeping the five practical ways to love your enemy in mind, discuss what you could have done differently.

NOTES

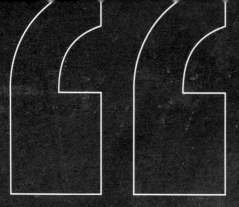

Be careful not to do your 'acts of righteousness' before others, to be seen by them. If you do, you will have no reward from your Father in heaven.

So when you give to the needy, do not announce it with trumpets, as the hypocrites do in the synagogues and on the streets, to be honored by others. I tell you the truth, they have received their reward in full.

But when you give to the needy, do not let your left hand know what your right hand is doing, so that your giving may be in secret. Then your Father, who sees what is done in secret, will reward you.

MATTHEW
6:1-4

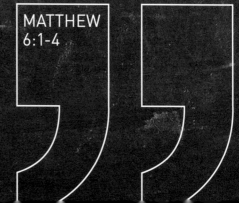

# how to **become** a **generous** **giver**

## INTRODUCTION

Jesus talks about our life 'below the waterline'; **our secret life with God**. There must be more weight below the water line than above.

We have to build our secret, hidden life with God.

The first area Jesus addresses is our giving.

# 1 BE CONVERTED

# 2 BUILD YOUR SECRET LIFE WITH GOD

**ff** ... when you give ... **JJ**

**MATTHEW 6:2**

Jesus assumes that if you are a Christian, you will give. It is part of the Christian life.

Martin Luther said that three conversions take place when we come to Christ: the conversion of the mind, the conversion of the heart and the conversion of the wallet.

Everything we have belongs to God; he is sharing it with us.

We are the stewards of God's gifts to us.

The New Testament lays down directions for how we are to use our money:

- give regularly **1 CORINTHIANS 16:2**
- give proportionately **2 CORINTHIANS 8:12**
- give generously **2 CORINTHIANS 9:6**
- give cheerfully **2 CORINTHIANS 9:7**

**ff** ... so that your giving may be in secret. **JJ**

**MATTHEW 6:4**

Jesus says that if we give secretly, then we will get our reward from God.

We need to know when it is appropriate to let our **ff light shine before others so that they may see your good works and glorify your Father in heaven JJ** and when to keep things secret from others.

**MATTHEW 5:16**

The distinction is in our motive; our motive should always be to glorify our Father in heaven.

**ff** Hide when you're tempted to show, and show when you're tempted to hide. **JJ**

This attitude applies to all our giving, whether we are giving money or time.

#GIVING

# 3 BECOME MORE LIKE GOD

# 4 BENEFIT FROM GOD'S REWARD

**" ... your Father in heaven ... "**
**MATTHEW 6:1**

What is God's attitude?

**" God so loved the world that he gave his one and only Son, so that whoever believes in him shall not die but have everlasting life. "**

**JOHN 3:16**

God's motive for giving is always love.

Giving is a way for us to become more like God; it is the path to holiness.

**" Then your Father ... will reward you. "**
**MATTHEW 6:4**

Jesus tells us that the very best investment we can make is to give.

Giving is like planting a seed: if we keep it, it will die. If we plant it, it will multiply.

Jesus says:
**" Give, and it will be given to you. A good measure, pressed down, shaken together and running over, will be poured into your lap. "**
**LUKE 6:38**

**" Whoever sows sparingly will also reap sparingly, and whoever sows generously will also reap generously. "**
**2 CORINTHIANS 9:6**

**" The world of the generous gets larger and larger; the world of the stingy gets smaller and smaller. "**
**PROVERBS 11:24, THE MESSAGE**

#GIVING

# 4 BENEFIT FROM GOD'S REWARD (CONTINUED)

# 5 BEGIN TO CHANGE THE WORLD AROUND YOU

There is no greater satisfaction than seeing the fruit of generous giving – in transformed lives.

**"**Giving cleans the heart and helps you get closer to God. **"**

*Mother Teresa*

**"**... when you give to the needy ... **"**
**MATTHEW 6:2**

Meeting people's needs changes lives.

We need a change of heart towards the church.

**"**The local church is the hope for the world. **"**

*Bill Hybels*

The church is best placed to do something about global poverty, preventable diseases and AIDS. It is the hope for the world in terms of healthcare, crime and education.

GIVING

# ONCLUSION

❝ Find a work of God you think you can trust, and give generously to it. Don't ration it. ❞
*Bishop Sandy Millar*

You do not have to be rich to give, just give what you can.

NOTES

# DISCUSSION QUESTIONS

**1.** If you give already, are you happy with how much you give and how often you do so, or do you feel that you need to re-think your priorities with regards to giving?

**2.** Why is it so important to 'not let your left hand know what your right hand is doing, so that your giving may be in secret' (Matthew 6:2-4)?

**3.** How do we change the world when we 'give to the needy' (Matthew 6:2)? How does our giving impact those around us? In which ways can our giving benefit society?

**4.** What are the benefits of giving for the givers?

**5.** Should people who don't have much themselves be expected to give? How can they manage this? Does the amount you give affect how 'your Father, who sees what is done in secret, will reward you' (Matthew 6:4)?

**6.** Aside from money, what other things we can give? Our time, our home, our friendship? Are these less important, equally important or more important than money? What does Jesus teach? What do you prefer to give?

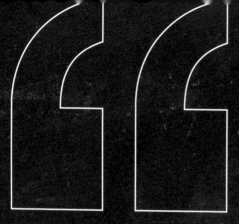

## PRAYER

And when you pray, do not be like the hypocrites, for they love to pray standing in the synagogues and on the street corners to be seen by others. I tell you the truth, they have received their reward in full. But when you pray, go into your room, close the door and pray to your Father, who is unseen. Then your Father, who sees what is done in secret, will reward you. And when you pray, do not keep on babbling like pagans, for they think they will be heard because of their many words. Do not be like them, for your Father knows what you need before you ask him. This, then, is how you should pray:

'Our Father in heaven,
hallowed be your name,
your kingdom come,
your will be done
on earth as it is in heaven.
Give us today our daily bread.

Forgive us our debts,
as we also have forgiven our debtors.
And lead us not into temptation,
but deliver us from the evil one.'

For if you forgive men when they sin against you, your heavenly Father will also forgive you. But if you do not forgive men their sins, your Father will not forgive your sins.

## FASTING

When you fast, do not look sombre as the hypocrites do, for they disfigure their faces to show others they are fasting. I tell you the truth, they have received their reward in full. But when you fast, put oil on your head and wash your face, so that it will not be obvious to others that you are fasting, but only to your Father, who is unseen; and your Father, who sees what is done in secret, will reward you.

MATTHEW
6:5-18

# How to
# pray (and fast) like Jesus

# INTRODUCTION

According to a recent survey, 73 per cent of people in London pray. **But are we really communicating with God?**

For many people prayer is a last resort, for use only in emergencies.

But according to Jesus, **prayer is key to our lives**. It is a means of communicating with God and building the relationship for which we were created.

❝ Prayer is nothing else than being on terms of friendship with God. ❞ *St Teresa of Avila (1515-1582)*

❝ Prayer is simply talking to God.
He speaks to us: we listen.
We speak to him: he listens.
A two-way process: speaking and listening. ❞
*Mother Teresa*

**How can we pray like Jesus?**

# 1 EXAMINE YOUR PRIORITIES

## PRAYER

Three times Jesus says: **" when you pray... "**            **MATTHEW 6:5-7**

Prayer was the number one priority for Jesus.

Stephen Covey, author of *The 7 Habits of Highly Effective People*, says, 'The key is not to prioritise what's on our schedules, but to schedule our priorities.'

If we can make prayer our first priority in the morning, it makes a huge difference to the day ahead.

## FASTING

Jesus says: **" When you fast ... "**            **MATTHEW 6:16-18**

We read of Jesus fasting on at least one occasion, but references in the Bible to fasting are relatively rare in comparison to prayer.

For some people it is not wise to fast.

But there can be spiritual benefits to fasting, including:

1. Strengthening and reinforcing prayer
            **MATTHEW 4:2**

2. Sign of repentance and humility before God            **DANIEL 9**

3. Seeking God's guidance            **ACTS 13:2**

4. Self-discipline
            **1 CORINTHIANS 9:24-27**

5. Sharing food with the hungry
            **ISAIAH 58:6-10**

In the New Testament, fasting means going without food for spiritual reasons. We can also be more imaginative about fasting, for example, giving up TV, the internet or shopping.

Whether praying and fasting, or just praying, **" your Father, who sees what is done in secret, will reward you. "**
            **MATTHEW 6:6 AND 18**

NOTES

# 1 EXAMINE YOUR PRIORITIES (CONTINUED)

# 2 ENJOY THE PRIVILEGE

The hidden rewards of prayer are **" too numerous to enumerate. "**

*John Stott*

As we pray, we experience God's love, as well as his joy and peace. We receive God's guidance and power for the day ahead.

PRAYER

1. Keep it real

**" And when you pray, do not be like the hypocrites, for they love to pray standing in the synagogues and on the street corners to be seen by others. I tell you the truth, they have received their reward in full. "**
**MATTHEW 6:5**

**" When you fast, do not look sombre as the hypocrites do, for they disfigure their faces to show others they are fasting. "**
**MATTHEW 6:16**

Jesus is not criticising public worship or corporate prayer, but he says we should not worship publicly to impress others. Rather, our motive should be to encounter God.

**" May it be the real I who speaks. "**
*C.S. Lewis*

There need be no pretence with God. We should make our prayers real, honest and authentic.

# 2
## ENJOY THE PRIVILEGE (CONTINUED)

# 3
## ESTABLISH A PATTERN

### 2. Keep it quiet

**❝ But when you pray, go into your room, close the door and pray to your Father, who is unseen. Then your Father, who sees what is done in secret, will reward you. ❞**                    **MATTHEW 6:6**

Not 'quiet' as opposed to 'loud', but 'quiet' as opposed to 'ostentatious'.

Jesus went to the mountains to pray. Find a quiet place so that you can pray without distractions.

### 3. Keep it simple

**❝ And when you pray, do not keep on babbling like pagans, for they think they will be heard because of their many words. Do not be like them, for your Father knows what you need before you ask him. ❞**            **MATTHEW 6:7-8**

We should be persistent in prayer, but it must come from the heart and it must be real.

One of the obstacles to prayer is not knowing how to pray. But Jesus shows us:
**❝ This, then, is how you should pray. ❞**
**MATTHEW 6:9**

For example:

Begin with thanksgiving and praise –
**❝ Our Father in heaven, ❞**
**MATTHEW 6:9**

Focus on God's honour –
**❝ hallowed be your name, ❞**
**MATTHEW 6:9**

Pray for God's rule and reign –
**❝ your kingdom come, ❞**
**MATTHEW 6:10**

Commit your decisions to God –
**❝ your will be done, on earth as it is in heaven. ❞**
**MATTHEW 6:10**

Ask for his help with daily needs –
**❝ Give us today our daily bread. ❞**
**MATTHEW 6:11**

# 3

## ESTABLISH A PATTERN
## (CONTINUED)

# CONCLUSIO

Make a clean start each day –
**❝ Forgive us our debts, ❞**
**MATTHEW 6:12**

Forgive anyone you need to forgive –
**❝ As we have forgiven our debtors...**
For if you forgive others when they sin
against you, your heavenly Father will
also forgive you. But if you do not forgive
others their sins, your Father will not
forgive your sins. ❞
**MATTHEW 6:12 AND 14**

Ask for his protection and power –

**❝ And lead us not into temptation,**
But deliver us from the evil one. ❞
**MATTHEW 6:13**

It is not always easy to pray: there are
distractions, sometimes prayers do
not get answered, and sometimes it
seems that God is far away.

But prayer is not a waste of time.

## ❝ WHEN I PRAY, COINCIDENCES HAPPEN. WHEN I DON'T, THEY DON'T. ❞
*William Temple*

Prayer **changes our lives** and it
**changes the world**.

We need to make prayer the **number
one priority** in our lives.

### RECOMMENDED READING LIST

*Prayer* – Philip Yancey

*God on Mute* – Pete Greig

*Too Busy Not to Pray* – Bill Hybels

# DISCUSSION QUESTIONS

**1.** Do you think that the time we spend praying reflects the priority of prayer in our lives? How do you decide what to prioritise in prayer?

**2.** How often do you find time to pray? Do you already keep it 'real', 'quiet' and 'simple'? If not, how can you begin to introduce these characteristics into your prayers?

**3.** Have you ever fasted? How did it affect your prayer time? Would you fast again? What would you do differently?

**4.** Do you regularly pray using the 'pattern' of The Lord's Prayer? Which are the parts you most need to focus on (eg: praising God, forgiveness, etc)?

**5.** We read in Matthew that 'when you pray' and 'when you fast', 'your Father, who sees what is done in secret, will reward you'. What does this mean? As Christians, how can we ensure that this is how we go about our praying and fasting?

**6.** How can we learn to pray more like Jesus? Do you think 'babbling like pagans' who 'think they will be heard because of their many words' is a common problem among Christians today?

NOTES

*Do not store up for yourselves treasures on earth, where moth and rust destroy, and where thieves break in and steal. But store up for yourselves treasures in heaven, where moth and rust do not destroy, and where thieves do not break in and steal. For where your treasure is, there your heart will be also.*

*The eye is the lamp of the body. If your eyes are good, your whole body will be full of light. But if your eyes are bad, your whole body will be full of darkness. If then the light within you is darkness, how great is that darkness!*

*No one can serve two masters. Either you will hate the one and love the other, or you will be devoted to the one and despise the other. You cannot serve both God and money.*

MATTHEW
6:19-24

# how to **handle** **ambition**

# INTRODUCTION

Our ambitions are the things we most want to achieve in life. Ambition can be good; it brings **purpose** and **aim**. But we need to have the right ambitions.

The wrong ambitions are **selfish ambitions**: building our treasure on earth and pursuing idols.

Twenty-first century idols include:

- **Money** divorced from reality

- **Sex** divorced from love

- **Fame** divorced from achievement

Affluenza: **"** Buying things we don't need, with money we haven't got, to satisfy needs that can't be satisfied by material things alone. **"**

*Oliver James*

How do we **avoid idolatry**? How can we be ambitious in the right way?

# INVEST YOUR LIFE FOR A HIGH RETURN

Jesus presents two possible ways of being secure, and calls us to an undivided heart:

**❝Do not store up for yourselves treasures on earth, where moth and rust destroy, and where thieves break in and steal. ❞**
**MATTHEW 6:19**

- Are we required to give away all we have? **MARK 10:21**, but see, for example, **MATTHEW 27:57** and **LUKE 8:1-3**

- Is it wrong to enjoy the good things of life? **1 TIMOTHY 6:17, LUKE 11:37, JOHN 2:1-11**

- Is it wrong to invest or to make money? For example, **MATTHEW 25:14-30**

- Is it wrong to save? **PROVERBS 21:20, 1 TIMOTHY 5:8, MARK 7:9-12**

**❝But store up for yourselves treasures in heaven, where moth and rust do not destroy, and where thieves do not break in and steal. For where your treasure is, there your heart will be also. ❞**
**MATTHEW 6:20-21**

Jesus is not concerned with our wealth, but with our hearts and affections. The New Testament does not attack money, but the love of money: **❝For the love of money is a root of all kinds of evil. ❞**
**1 TIMOTHY 6:10**

If our treasure is on earth, our heart will be tethered to the earth.

We can invest in the kingdom of God in many different ways, for example:

- Preaching the Gospel

- Bringing up children as followers of Jesus Christ

- Working at family life

- Helping the homeless

Investing our treasure in heaven is totally secure and will last forever.

# 2 FIX YOUR EYES IN THE RIGHT DIRECTION

Jesus puts before us two possible visions for our life and calls us to be single-minded:

**❝ The eye is the lamp of the body. If your eyes are good, your whole body will be full of light. But if your eyes are bad, your whole body will be full of darkness. If then the light within you is darkness, how great is that darkness! ❞**
**MATTHEW 6:22-23**

Where do we set our spiritual eyes? On God or on greed?

A bad eye is set on selfish gain and materialism. It leads to darkness.

A good eye is looking in the right direction. Everything else follows behind.

**❝ Let us fix our eyes on Jesus ... ❞**
**HEBREWS 12:2**

- Daily
- Weekly

# 3 SPEND YOUR TIME WORKING FOR A LIBERATING BOSS

Jesus offers us two possible gods and calls us to a surrendered will:

**❝ No one can serve two masters. Either he will hate the one and love the other, or he will be devoted to the one and despise the other. You cannot serve both God and money. ❞**
**MATTHEW 6:24**

Money demands human sacrifice. It is a good servant, but a terrible master.

Materialism is a form of atheism.

If we are working for God, we will hold money lightly. We will be materially satisfied and we will see ourselves as stewards of the money we have.

# ONCLUSION

In order to break the power of materialism, we need to give generously.

Every time we give, we are declaring that Jesus is Lord and money is not.

## THE SOLUTION IS TO **"** FIX OUR EYES ON JESUS. **"**

### RECOMMENDED READING

*God At Work* – Ken Costa

*Everything Must Change* – Brian McLaren

If you are (or someone you know is) struggling with debt and would like some advice, please call Christians Against Poverty (CAP) on 0800 328 0006 to make an appointment to see a debt advisor, visit www.capuk.org or email infocapuk.org

NOTES

# DISCUSSION QUESTIONS

**1.** Which things in your life are vying to be your heart's 'treasure' (Matthew 6:21)?

**2.** What kind of things, according to the Bible, might be considered positive 'treasures'? What might be considered negative ones? How can we keep the right things as the most important things in our lives?

**3.** How do you think things would change in society if money became less of a 'master' (Matthew 6:24). How can we, as Christians, help to bring about a change in the way people view money?

**4.** How does 'fix[ing] our eyes on Jesus' (Hebrews 12:2) help us to 'store up … treasures in heaven' (Matthew 6:20)? Why is this so important to do? How can we make sure we do this?

**5.** Think of a time when money (or another worldly 'treasure') felt more important to you than your relationship with God. How did you recognise the signs? What did you do? Is this particular treasure still a source of difficulty for you?

**6.** Is it difficult to find a balance between being ambitious, successful and maximising your savings and keeping your eyes, and your focus, on Jesus (Hebrews 12:2)? How do you currently manage it? How could you deal with this more effectively?

**7.** What does success mean for you? What, in your eyes, makes a person successful?

**THE JESUS LIFESTYLE**